NARWHALS

Unicorns of the Sea

COLOURING BOOK

Christina Rose

NARWHALS Unicorns of the Sea
COLOURING BOOK

ISBN: 978-1-912511-15-0

Created by Christina Rose

Contributors: Frances Coles, Shutterstock

BELL & MACKENZIE
PUBLISHING LIMITED
www.bellmackenzie.com

Unicorns of the Sea

Unicorns of the Sea

Unicorns of the Sea

Unicorns of the Sea

Unicorns of the Sea

Unicorns of the Sea

Unicorns of the Sea

Unicorns of the Sea

Unicorns of the Sea

Unicorns of the Sea

Unicorns of the Sea

Unicorns of the Sea

Unicorns of the Sea

Unicorns of the Sea

Unicorns of the Sea

Unicorns of the Sea

Unicorns of the Sea

Unicorns of the Sea

Unicorns of the Sea

Unicorns of the Sea

Unicorns of the Sea

Unicorns of the Sea

Unicorns of the Sea

Unicorns of the Sea

Unicorns of the Sea

Unicorns of the Sea

Unicorns of the Sea

BLAH BLAH BLAH BLAH
BLAH BLAH BLAH BLAH BLAH
BLAH BLAH BLAH BLAH BLAH
GRUMPY

Unicorns of the Sea

Unicorns of the Sea

Unicorns of the Sea

Unicorns of the Sea

Unicorns of the Sea

Unicorns of the Sea

Unicorns of the Sea

Unicorns of the Sea

Unicorns of the Sea

Unicorns of the Sea

Unicorns of the Sea

Unicorns of the Sea

Unicorns of the Sea

Unicorns of the Sea

Unicorns of the Sea

Unicorns of the Sea

Made in United States
Orlando, FL
03 May 2022

17458472R00054